The

Incredible

Florida Carpenter Ant

Understanding their special amputation process,

Unique Physical Characteristics for identification,

and effective methods to get rid of them

Anthony Lawrence

Table of Contents

Introduction

The Fascinating World of Florida Carpenter Ants

Florida carpenter ants (Camponotus floridanus) are among the most intriguing insect species in the animal kingdom. Known for their distinctive red and black coloring, these ants inhabit various moist environments, from attics and ceilings to trees and woodpiles. Despite their name, carpenter ants do not eat wood but excavate it to create elaborate nests, causing significant structural damage over time.

What sets Florida carpenter ants apart from other ant species is not just their nesting habits or diet but their recently discovered medical behavior. These ants have been observed performing life-saving amputations on their injured nestmates, showcasing a level of medical sophistication previously unseen in the animal kingdom. This remarkable behavior has opened new avenues of research and added to the growing body of knowledge about the complex social structures and survival strategies of ants.

Importance of Studying Carpenter Ants

Studying Florida carpenter ants is crucial for several reasons. Firstly, their unique amputation behavior provides invaluable insights into the evolutionary adaptations and social dynamics of insects. Understanding how these ants diagnose and treat injuries can inform broader biological and medical research, potentially leading to innovations in human medical treatments.

Secondly, carpenter ants play a significant role in their ecosystems. As both predators and prey, they influence the populations of other insects and contribute to the ecological balance. By studying their behavior and interactions, scientists can gain a deeper understanding of ecosystem dynamics and the importance of biodiversity.

Moreover, Florida carpenter ants are a common pest in many homes and buildings, particularly in areas with high moisture levels. Their nesting activities can cause substantial property damage, making it essential for homeowners and pest control professionals to understand their behavior, nesting preferences, and effective methods for controlling infestations.

Finally, the study of carpenter ants highlights the incredible diversity within the ant family. With over 12,000 known species, ants exhibit a wide range of behaviors, adaptations, and survival strategies. By focusing on the specific traits of Florida carpenter ants, researchers can compare them with other species, uncovering the broader patterns and unique characteristics that define ant biology.

In summary, the study of Florida carpenter ants is not only fascinating but also crucial for advancing our understanding of insect behavior, ecosystem health, and pest management.

This book aims to explore these remarkable creatures in-depth, shedding light on their unique medical practices and providing comprehensive information on their biology, behavior, and interactions with humans.

Remarkable Medical Discoveries

The Discovery of Amputation Behavior

In a groundbreaking discovery, researchers have documented a medical behavior in Florida carpenter ants (Camponotus floridanus) that has never been seen before in the animal kingdom: amputations performed by the ants on their injured nestmates. This behavior, akin to battlefield triage in human warfare, demonstrates an advanced level of social cooperation and medical intervention that challenges our understanding of insect behavior.

The discovery was made by behavioral ecologists who observed that when Florida carpenter ants sustain injuries during conflicts with neighboring colonies, their fellow ants undertake a medical procedure to amputate the damaged limb. This process significantly increases the survival rate of the injured ants, highlighting a sophisticated approach to wound management and care within the colony.

Analyzing the Amputation Treatment: How It Is Done

The amputation process in Florida carpenter ants begins with the diagnosis of the injury. Researchers have noted that the ants can distinguish between injuries that require amputation and those that do not. If the injury is located further up the leg, particularly at the femur, the ants proceed with the amputation. However, if the wound is lower down the leg, they opt for obsessive grooming instead, likely to remove pathogens and prevent infection.

The actual amputation is a cooperative effort between the injured ant and its nestmates. The injured ant presents its damaged leg to the others, seemingly willing to undergo the procedure. The assisting ants then bite ferociously at the injured limb, severing it from the body. Despite the apparent violence of the act, the injured remains cooperative, indicating a possible understanding of the necessity of the procedure for its survival.

Case Studies and Observations

Several case studies have documented the amputation behavior in detail. For example, in one observation, an injured and severely damaged femur was seen presenting its leg to a group of worker ants. Over several minutes, the workers bit at the leg until it was completely severed. The injured then received further grooming and care from their nestmates, increasing their chances of recovery.

In another case, an ant with a lower leg injury did not undergo amputation but was instead groomed meticulously by its fellow ants. This grooming process involved the ants using their mouthparts to clean the wound, likely to prevent infection. The survival rate for ants receiving such grooming treatment was significantly higher than for those left untreated.

These observations highlight not only the amputation behavior but also the ants' ability to adapt their medical responses based on the type and location of the injury.

This adaptability is a testament to the complex social structure and communication within the colony.

Comparison with Other Animal Medical Behaviors

The medical behaviors of Florida carpenter ants stand out when compared to other known examples in the animal kingdom. While many animals exhibit self-care behaviors, such as grooming or using natural substances to treat wounds, the deliberate amputation of limbs by Florida carpenter ants is unique.

For instance, certain primates like chimpanzees and orangutans have been observed applying poultices to their wounds, and lemurs use chewed-up millipedes as an anti-parasitic treatment. Honeybees line their hives with antimicrobial plant compounds to protect against infections. However, these behaviors generally involve self-treatment or preventive measures, rather than the cooperative surgical intervention seen in Florida carpenter ants.

Another notable example is the termite-hunting Matabele ant (Megaponera analis), which has been observed treating its wounds with antimicrobial compounds produced by a specialized gland. However, unlike Florida carpenter ants, Matabele ants do not perform amputations.

The amputation behavior of Florida carpenter ants showcases a level of medical care that involves accurate diagnosis, cooperative execution, and post-treatment care, distinguishing it as a remarkable and unprecedented behavior in the animal world. This discovery not only broadens our understanding of insect social structures but also provides a fascinating glimpse into the evolution of medical practices in the natural world.

BASIC BIOLOGY OF FLORIDA CARPENTER ANTS

Basic Biology of Florida Carpenter Ants

Physical Characteristics

Florida carpenter ants (Camponotus floridanus) are easily recognizable due to their distinct bicolored appearance. They possess a reddish-orange thorax and a black abdomen, giving them a striking contrast. Adult workers typically measure between 6 to 12 millimeters in length, with queens being larger, sometimes exceeding 20 millimeters.

Their bodies are divided into three segments: the head, thorax, and abdomen, with the thorax being notably large and robust. Florida carpenter ants have powerful mandibles used for excavating wood and defending the colony. They lack a sting but can bite and spray formic acid as a defense mechanism. Their antennae are segmented and bent, providing them with a heightened sense of smell and touch, essential for communication and navigation.

Life Cycle and Lifespan

The life cycle of Florida carpenter ants begins with a mating flight, typically occurring during the spring swarm season between April and June. Winged males and females leave their nests to mate in the air. After mating, the males die, and the fertilized females, now queens, seek out suitable locations to establish new colonies.

Once a queen finds a nesting site, she sheds her wings and begins laying eggs. The first brood of eggs develops into worker ants, who then take over the responsibilities of foraging, caring for the queen's subsequent offspring, and expanding the nest. The colony grows over several years, with the queen continuing to lay eggs throughout her life.

The lifespan of a Florida carpenter ant varies by caste. Queens can live for several years, sometimes up to a decade, while worker ants typically live for a few months to a couple of years. Male ants, whose sole purpose is to mate, live only for a short period, often just a few weeks.

Seasonal Behavior and Activity

Florida carpenter ants exhibit distinct seasonal behaviors that are closely tied to their life cycle and environmental conditions. Their activity is most noticeable during the warmer months, particularly in spring and summer, when they are actively foraging and expanding their nests.

During the spring swarm season, usually from April to June, winged reproductive ants are frequently seen inside homes, along window ledges, and near sliding glass doors, often mistaken for termites. This is a critical period for the species as it is when new colonies are established.

In the summer, the ants are highly active, foraging for food to support their growing colonies. They primarily forage at night, with peak activity occurring just before sunset until two hours after sunset, and again around dawn. Their foraging trails are loosely defined, often appearing as random wandering.

As the weather cools in the fall and winter, the ants' activity diminishes. They remain relatively inactive during colder months, focusing on maintaining their nests and conserving resources until warmer temperatures return.

Understanding the basic biology of Florida carpenter ants, including their physical characteristics, life cycle, and seasonal behavior, is essential for effective management and control, as well as for appreciating the complexities of their social structures and survival strategies.

Habitat and Nesting Habits

Preferred Nesting Locations

Florida carpenter ants (Camponotus floridanus) exhibit a preference for nesting in areas with high moisture levels, which provide the ideal conditions for their colonies to thrive. They are commonly found in decayed or hollow wood, where they can excavate extensive networks of tunnels and chambers. Moisture-rich environments such as attics, ceilings, windows, doors, trees, shrubs, woodpiles, plumbing and electrical entries, gutters, vents, trashcans, and even sheds or doghouses are typical nesting sites. These locations offer protection from environmental changes and predators, ensuring a stable environment for the colony's growth and development.

Nesting in Natural and Human-Made Structures

In natural settings, Florida carpenter ants prefer nesting in partially decayed wood and moist areas. They can be found in tree trunks, branches, stumps, and logs, where they excavate their nests without consuming the wood.

Instead, they hollow it out to create smooth tunnels and galleries. This behavior, while natural, can contribute to the decay and breakdown of dead trees, playing a role in the ecosystem by recycling nutrients back into the soil.

In human-made structures, however, their nesting habits can cause significant issues. Florida carpenter ants are notorious for invading homes and buildings, particularly in areas where moisture problems exist. Attics, ceilings, and walls made of wood are prime targets for these ants. They also commonly nest around windows and doors, where moisture can accumulate, as well as in plumbing and electrical entries. The ants do not eat the wood but remove it to expand their nests, leading to structural damage over time.

Impact on the Environment and Human Habitations

Florida carpenter ants have a dual impact on the environment and human habitation. In natural environments, they contribute to the ecosystem by breaking down dead wood, which aids in nutrient cycling and decomposition processes. This activity helps maintain the health of forests and other natural habitats by promoting the growth of new vegetation.

However, in human habitations, their nesting behavior poses a significant threat. The structural damage caused by their excavation activities can be severe, particularly when they infest wooden components of buildings. Their tunneling can eventually damage the integrity of hardwood beams, floors, and other structural parts, perhaps resulting in costly repairs. Moist areas such as basements, crawl spaces, and attics are especially vulnerable to infestation, as the ants are drawn to these environments.

In addition to structural damage, Florida carpenter ants can become a nuisance due to their foraging behavior. They are attracted to sweets and other food sources, which can lead them into kitchens and other living areas. Their presence can be unsettling, and their bites, although not dangerous, can cause discomfort due to the injection of formic acid.

Effective management of Florida carpenter ant infestations involves addressing moisture issues, sealing entry points, and employing targeted treatments to eliminate nests. Understanding their preferred nesting locations and behaviors is crucial for preventing and mitigating the impact of these ants on human structures while appreciating their ecological role in natural environments.

Diet and Foraging Behavior

Typical Diet: What Do They Eat?

Florida carpenter ants (Camponotus floridanus) have a diverse and adaptable diet that includes both plant and animal matter. Their omnivorous feeding habits allow them to exploit a wide range of food sources, ensuring the survival and growth of their colonies. Their diet consists of:

1. Sugary Substances: Florida carpenter ants have a strong preference for sweets. They are particularly attracted to honeydew, a sugary excretion produced by aphids and other plant-sucking insects. This substance is a major component of their diet and provides essential carbohydrates for energy. In addition to honeydew, they also consume nectar from flowers and other sugary substances they encounter in their environment.

2. Living and Dead Insects: As opportunistic feeders, Florida carpenter ants prey on small insects and arthropods. They capture and consume live insects, which provide the protein necessary for the growth and development of their larvae. They also scavenge on dead insects, which are easier to collect and transport back to the nest.

3. Household Foods: Inside human habitations, Florida carpenter ants forage for a variety of foods. They are particularly attracted to sugary foods such as candies, syrups, and fruits. They also consume proteins and fats found in meats, pet food, and grease. Their foraging behavior can lead them into kitchens, pantries, and other areas where food is stored or prepared.

4. Plant Material: While not a primary food source, Florida carpenter ants may consume parts of plants, such as fruits and seeds, when available. This behavior is more common in natural settings where they forage on vegetation.

Foraging Patterns and Schedules

Florida carpenter ants exhibit distinct foraging patterns and schedules that maximize their efficiency in gathering food while minimizing the risk of predation and environmental hazards. Key aspects of their foraging behavior include:

1. Nocturnal Activity: These ants are primarily nocturnal foragers, meaning they are most active during the night. Foraging typically begins just before sunset and continues for a few hours after sunset. They have another peak of activity around dawn. This nocturnal behavior helps them avoid the heat of the day and reduce the likelihood of encountering predators.

2. Loosely Defined Trails: Unlike some ant species that follow strict and well-defined foraging trails, Florida carpenter ants often forage along loosely defined trails or wander individually. This seemingly aimless wandering allows them to cover a larger area and increases their chances of encountering food sources.

3. Nest-to-Food Source Communication: Once a foraging ant finds a food source, it communicates the location to other members of the colony. This communication can involve the use of pheromones, which are chemical signals that guide other ants to the food. However, the recruitment of other foragers is less intense compared to some other ant species, resulting in smaller numbers of ants at any given food source.

4. Adaptability: Florida carpenter ants are highly adaptable in their foraging habits. They can switch between different types of food sources depending on availability. This adaptability ensures a steady supply of nutrients for the colony, even when certain food sources become scarce.

Interaction with Other Species for Food

Florida carpenter ants interact with various other species in their quest for food, forming complex ecological relationships. Some of these interactions include:

1. Mutualism with Aphids: One of the most well-known interactions is their mutualistic relationship with aphids and other honeydew-producing insects. The ants protect these insects from predators and parasites, and in return, they harvest the honeydew produced by the aphids. This mutually beneficial relationship ensures a continuous supply of sugary food for the ants.

2. Competition with Other Ant Species: Florida carpenter ants often compete with other ant species for food resources. This competition can lead to aggressive encounters and territorial disputes. They may engage in battles with other colonies of the same species or different species to defend their foraging territories and access to food sources.

3. Predation on Other Insects: As predators, Florida carpenter ants hunt and capture various insects and arthropods. This predation helps regulate the populations of their prey species and can impact the local insect community. Their role as predators contributes to the overall balance of the ecosystem.

4. Interactions with Human Activities: In human environments, Florida carpenter ants are often attracted to food waste, spills, and improperly stored food. They can become pests in homes, restaurants, and other buildings where food is present. Their foraging behavior brings them into contact with humans, leading to efforts to control and manage their populations to prevent infestations.

Understanding the diet and foraging behavior of Florida carpenter ants provides valuable insights into their ecological role and the strategies they use to sustain their colonies. Their adaptability and complex interactions with other species highlight the intricate dynamics of their existence and the impact they have on both natural and human-modified environments.

Infestations and Their Implications

Signs of Infestation

Detecting an infestation of Florida carpenter ants (Camponotus floridanus) early is crucial for preventing extensive damage to structures and property. Some common signs of infestation include:

1. Visible Ant Activity: The presence of large, reddish-black ants, especially in moist or damp areas, is a strong indicator of an infestation. These ants are often seen foraging in kitchens, bathrooms, and other areas where food and moisture are present.

2. Sawdust or Frass: Carpenter ants do not eat wood but excavate it to create their nests. This activity produces sawdust-like material known as frass, which may include wood shavings, insect parts, and other debris. Frass can often be found near nest entrances or below infested wooden structures.

3. Winged Ants: The appearance of winged carpenter ants, particularly during the spring swarm season from

April to June, is a sign that a colony is established nearby. These reproductive ants, or alates, emerge to mate and start new colonies, often leading to the spread of infestations.

4. Hollow-Sounding Wood: Tapping on wooden structures that sound hollow can indicate the presence of carpenter ant nests. Their tunneling activities weaken the wood, creating voids that produce a distinct sound when tapped.

5. Rustling Noises: In quiet environments, faint rustling noises within walls or wooden structures can be heard as the ants move and excavate wood.

6. Moisture Problems: Areas with persistent moisture issues, such as leaky roofs, plumbing leaks, or poor ventilation, are prone to carpenter ant infestations. Inspecting these locations regularly can help detect infestations early.

Impact on Structures and Property

Florida carpenter ants can cause significant damage to structures and property through their nesting activities. Key impacts include:

1. Structural Damage: Carpenter ants excavate wood to create their nests, resulting in weakened structural integrity. Over time, their tunneling can cause extensive damage to wooden beams, floors, ceilings, and walls. This damage can compromise the safety and stability of buildings, leading to costly repairs.

2. Damage to Insulation and Wiring: In addition to wood, carpenter ants may also nest in insulation and around electrical wiring. This can lead to reduced insulation effectiveness and potential electrical hazards, including short circuits and fire risks.

3. Aesthetic Damage: Visible damage, such as holes in wood, frass accumulation, and ant trails, can detract from the aesthetic appeal of a property. This can be particularly concerning for homeowners and businesses aiming to maintain a clean and well-kept appearance.

4. Infestation Spread: Carpenter ants can establish multiple satellite colonies connected to the main nest. This behavior can result in infestations spreading throughout a property, making control efforts more challenging and increasing the potential for widespread damage.

Economic and Environmental Consequences

The economic and environmental consequences of Florida carpenter ant infestations are significant and multifaceted:

1. Economic Costs: The financial impact of carpenter ant infestations can be substantial. Costs associated with repairing structural damage, replacing infested wood, and addressing moisture issues can be high. Additionally, professional pest control services may be required to effectively eliminate infestations and prevent recurrence.

2. Property Value: Infestations can negatively affect property values. Potential buyers may be deterred by signs of infestation or the need for extensive repairs, leading to reduced marketability and lower sale prices. Regular inspections and prompt treatment of infestations are essential to maintain property value.

3. Business Disruption: For businesses, carpenter ant infestations can disrupt operations, particularly in sectors where cleanliness and hygiene are critical, such as food service and healthcare. Infestations may lead to temporary closures, loss of revenue, and damage to reputation.

4. Environmental Impact: While carpenter ants play a beneficial role in natural ecosystems by breaking down dead wood and contributing to nutrient cycling, their presence in human structures can lead to increased pesticide use. This can have unintended environmental consequences, including the potential impact on non-target species and the contamination of soil and water sources.

5. Health and Safety Concerns: Although carpenter ants do not transmit diseases, their bites can cause discomfort due to the injection of formic acid. Additionally, the structural damage they cause can create safety hazards, such as weakened floors and ceilings that may pose risks to occupants.

6. Preventive Measures: Addressing moisture problems, sealing entry points, and maintaining regular inspections are crucial preventive measures. Educating property owners and residents about the signs of infestation and the importance of early detection can help mitigate the economic and environmental impacts of carpenter ant infestations.

In conclusion, understanding the signs of Florida carpenter ant infestations, their impact on structures and property, and the broader economic and environmental consequences is essential for effective management and prevention. Proactive measures, timely interventions, and professional pest control services can help protect properties from the damaging effects of these industrious insects.

Interaction with Humans

Interaction with Humans

What to Do If Bitten

Florida carpenter ants (Camponotus floridanus) can bite when they feel threatened, although their bites are not generally dangerous to humans. If bitten by a Florida carpenter ant, here are the steps to take:

1. Remain Calm: Panic can exacerbate the situation. Staying calm will help you manage the bite more effectively.

2. Clean the Bite Area: Immediately wash the affected area with soap and water to prevent infection. This also helps to remove any formic acid the ant may have injected.

3. Apply an Antiseptic: After cleaning, apply an antiseptic solution or cream to the bite to further prevent infection.

4. Use a Cold Compress: To reduce swelling and alleviate pain, apply a cold compress or ice pack wrapped in a cloth to the bite area for about 10 minutes.

5. Over-the-counter Treatments: If there is significant discomfort, over-the-counter antihistamines can help reduce itching and swelling. Pain medications like acetaminophen or ibuprofen can help control pain.

6. Monitor for Allergic Reactions: While rare, some individuals may experience allergic reactions to ant bites. Symptoms can include difficulty breathing, swelling of the lips or throat, dizziness, or a rapid heartbeat. If any of these symptoms appear, get medical attention right away.

7. Avoid Scratching: Scratching the bite can introduce bacteria into the wound and cause infection. Try to keep the area clean and avoid scratching.

Health Implications of Bites

While Florida carpenter ant bites are generally not serious, there are a few health implications to be aware of:

1. Pain and Discomfort: The bite itself can be painful and may cause a sharp, stinging sensation. This is due to the ant's mandibles and the injection of formic acid, which can cause a burning feeling.

2. Swelling and Redness: The area around the bite may become red and swollen. This reaction is typically mild and localized.

3. Infection: If the bite area is not properly cleaned and cared for, it can become infected. Increased redness, warmth, swelling, and pus are all signs of infection. Infections require medical treatment, often with antibiotics.

4. Allergic Reactions: Although uncommon, some individuals may have allergic reactions to ant bites.

Symptoms of an allergic reaction can range from mild (itching, hives) to severe (anaphylaxis). Severe allergic reactions are medical emergencies and require immediate attention.

5. Long-Term Effects: Most ant bites heal without any long-term effects. However, in rare cases, individuals may develop persistent itching or discomfort at the bite site. Consult a healthcare practitioner to assist manage these symptoms.

Myths and Facts about Carpenter Ant Bites

There are several myths and misconceptions about carpenter ant bites. Understanding the facts can help dispel these myths and provide accurate information:

1. Myth: Carpenter Ants Inject Poisonous Venom

   - **Fact**: Unlike some other ants, carpenter ants do not have a venomous sting. They bite using their strong mandibles and may inject formic acid to irritate, but this acid is not poisonous.

2. Myth: Carpenter Ant Bites are Deadly

- **Fact**: Carpenter ant bites are not deadly. While they can cause discomfort and, in rare cases, allergic reactions, they are not life-threatening to the average person.

3. Myth: All Ant Bites Require Medical Attention

- **Fact**: Most ant bites, including those from carpenter ants, do not require medical attention. Basic first aid measures, such as cleaning the bite and applying a cold compress, are usually sufficient. Medical attention is only necessary if there are signs of an allergic reaction or infection.

4. Myth: Carpenter Ants Only Bite in Self-Defense

- **Fact**: While carpenter ants do bite in self-defense, they can also bite if they are disturbed or feel threatened. They are not aggressive by nature but will protect their nest if necessary.

5. Myth: Carpenter Ant Bites Leave Permanent Scars

- **Fact**: Carpenter ant bites typically do not leave permanent scars. Proper care and hygiene can prevent complications such as infections, which might otherwise lead to scarring.

6. Myth: Carpenter Ant Bites are as Dangerous as Fire Ant Stings

- **Fact**: Fire ants inject venom when they sting, which can cause intense pain, swelling, and even severe allergic reactions. In contrast, carpenter ants only bite and inject formic acid, which causes mild irritation in most cases.

7. Myth: You Can Prevent Bites by Eliminating All Ants

- **Fact**: While controlling ant populations can reduce the likelihood of bites, it is nearly impossible to eliminate all ants from an environment. Good pest control practices can minimize their presence indoors, reducing the risk of encounters.

Understanding the interaction between Florida carpenter ants and humans helps in managing and preventing bites, while also dispelling common myths. By taking appropriate steps when bitten and knowing the true risks and benefits associated with these ants, individuals can coexist more harmoniously with these fascinating insects.

Pest Control and Elimination

Pest Control and Elimination

Proven Methods to Get Rid of Florida Carpenter Ants

Effectively eliminating Florida carpenter ants (Camponotus floridanus) requires a combination of targeted treatments and preventive measures. Here are some proven methods:

1. Locate and Destroy Nests: Finding and treating nests directly is the most effective way to eliminate carpenter ants. Nests are often located in moist, decayed wood, inside walls, or in other hidden areas. Once located, nests can be treated with insecticidal dust or sprays specifically designed for carpenter ants.

2. Use Insecticidal Baits: Baits are an effective way to target the entire colony. Place baits along ant trails and near nest entrances. Worker ants carry the bait back to the nest, where it is shared with other colony members, including the queen. This method can take several days to weeks to be fully effective.

3. Apply Residual Insecticides: Use residual insecticides around the perimeter of your home, along ant trails, and in areas where ants are frequently seen. These products can provide long-lasting control by killing ants that come into contact with the treated surfaces.

4. Eliminate Moisture Sources: Carpenter ants are attracted to moisture. Fix any leaks in plumbing, roofs, or windows, and ensure proper ventilation in attics and crawl spaces. Reducing moisture can make your home less attractive to ants.

5. Seal Entry Points: Inspect your home for potential entry points, such as cracks in walls, gaps around windows and doors, and openings around utility lines. Seal these entry points with silicone caulk or other appropriate materials to prevent ants from entering.

6. Remove Food Sources: Carpenter ants are attracted to sugary and protein-rich foods. Keep food in sealed containers, clean up spills and crumbs promptly, and maintain a clean kitchen and dining area. Removing potential food sources can help deter ants.

7. Trim Vegetation: Ants often use branches and vegetation to access homes. Trim trees, shrubs, and other plants away from your home to eliminate these access routes.

8. Store Firewood Properly: Store firewood and other wooden materials away from your home and off the ground. Carpenter ants can nest in firewood, and storing it away from your home can help prevent infestations.

Prevention Tips for Homeowners

Preventing carpenter ant infestations involves continual awareness and preventive tactics. Here are some tips for homeowners:

1. Regular Inspections: Conduct regular inspections of your home, particularly in areas prone to moisture, such as basements, crawl spaces, attics, and plumbing. Look for signs of ant activity, such as frass, damaged wood, and ant trails.

2. Maintain a Clean Environment: Keep your home clean and free of food debris. Regularly clean floors, countertops, and other surfaces where food particles may accumulate. Store food in sealed containers and clean up any spills right away.

3. Proper Waste Management: Dispose of garbage regularly and keep trash cans clean and sealed. Carpenter ants are attracted to food waste and other organic materials.

4. Landscaping Maintenance: Maintain your yard and garden to minimize ant access to your home. Trim back trees and shrubs that touch your house, and keep the area around your home free of debris and woodpiles.

5. Monitor Moisture Levels: Address any moisture issues in your home. Ensure proper ventilation in high-humidity areas, use dehumidifiers if necessary, and repair leaks promptly.

6. Seal Cracks and Gaps: Regularly inspect and seal cracks, gaps, and other potential entry points around your home's exterior. Pay particular attention to areas around doors, windows, utility lines, and the foundation.

7. Professional Inspection: Consider having a professional pest control expert inspect your home annually. They can identify potential issues and provide recommendations for preventing infestations.

8. Educate Household Members: Inform everyone in your household about the importance of keeping the home clean and reporting any signs of ant activity immediately.

Professional Pest Control Solutions

When DIY methods are insufficient or when dealing with a severe infestation, professional pest control services can offer effective solutions:

1. Comprehensive Inspection: Pest control professionals conduct thorough inspections to locate nests, identify ant species, and assess the extent of the infestation. This allows for targeted and effective treatment plans.

2. Customized Treatment Plans: Professionals develop customized treatment plans based on the specific needs of your home and the severity of the infestation. These plans may include a combination of baits, insecticides, and exclusion techniques.

3. Advanced Treatment Methods: Pest control experts have access to advanced treatment methods and products that are not available to the general public. These products are often more effective and longer-lasting.

4. Safe and Effective Use of Pesticides: Professionals are trained to use pesticides safely and effectively, minimizing risks to humans, pets, and the environment. They can also guide how to avoid exposure to treated areas.

5. Integrated Pest Management (IPM): Many pest control companies employ Integrated Pest Management (IPM) strategies, which focus on long-term prevention through a combination of biological, mechanical, and chemical controls. IPM emphasizes reducing reliance on chemical treatments and promoting sustainable practices.

6. Ongoing Monitoring and Maintenance: Professional services often include ongoing monitoring and maintenance to ensure that the infestation is fully eliminated and to prevent future infestations. This may involve regular inspections and treatments as needed.

7. Expert Advice and Education: Pest control professionals can provide valuable advice and education on preventing future infestations. They can recommend specific actions to take, such as improving home maintenance practices and addressing environmental factors that attract ants.

8. Guarantees and Warranties: Many pest control companies offer guarantees or warranties for their services, providing peace of mind that the problem will be resolved. If the ants return within a certain period, the company will retreat to the area at no additional cost.

In conclusion, effectively managing Florida carpenter ant infestations requires a multifaceted approach that includes both preventive measures and targeted treatments. Homeowners can take proactive steps to reduce the risk of infestations, but professional pest control services offer the expertise and advanced solutions needed for comprehensive management and long-term prevention. By combining these strategies, it is possible to protect homes and properties from the damaging effects of carpenter ants.

Differentiating Carpenter Ants from Other Ants and Termites

Physical and Behavioral Differences

Physical Characteristics

Carpenter Ants (Camponotus floridanus):

- **Size**: Carpenter ants are among the largest ants, with workers ranging from 6 to 12 millimeters in length. The queen can be up to 20 millimeters long.

- **Color**: Florida carpenter ants are typically bicolored, with a reddish-brown or red thorax and a black abdomen. Some can be entirely black or dark brown.

- **Antennae**: They have bent or elbowed antennae.

- **Body Shape:** Carpenter ants have a distinct waist with one node (a small segment connecting the thorax and abdomen).

- **Wings:** Winged reproductive carpenter ants (alates) have two pairs of wings, with the front pair longer than the rear pair.

Other Ants:

- **Size and Color:** Other ant species vary widely in size and color. For instance, fire ants are smaller and reddish, while odorous house ants are small and brown.

- **Antennae and Waist:** Like carpenter ants, other ants also have elbowed antennae. However, many species have a different number of nodes (one or two) in their waist.

- **Wings:** Winged forms of other ants also have two pairs of wings, with similar proportions to carpenter ants.

Termites:

- **Size:** Termites are generally smaller than carpenter ants, with workers about 3 to 4 millimeters long. The reproductive individuals are larger, and similar in size to carpenter ants.

- **Color:** Termites are usually pale, ranging from white to light brown.

- **Antennae:** Termites have straight, beaded antennae.

- **Body Shape:** Termites have a broad waist without any noticeable segmentation.

- **Wings**: Winged termites (swarmers) have two pairs of wings of equal length, which are longer than their bodies and have a straight, uniform vein pattern.

Behavioral Characteristics

Carpenter Ants:

- **Nesting Habits:** Carpenter ants nest in wood but do not consume it. They hollow out sections of wood to create smooth galleries.

- **Foraging Behavior:** They forage primarily at night and follow loosely defined trails. Their diet includes sweets, meats, and other household foods.

- **Colony Structure:** Carpenter ant colonies can be extensive, often having multiple satellite nests in addition to a main nest.

Other Ants:

- **Nesting Habits:** Vary widely. Some nest in soil, under rocks, in decayed wood, or within household structures.

- **Foraging Behavior:** Many ants forage both day and night. Their diet and foraging patterns depend on the species.

- **Colony Structure:** Also varies. Some species have smaller colonies, while others, like Argentine ants, form massive supercolonies.

Termites:

- **Nesting Habits:** Termites consume wood, creating a network of tunnels within it. They live within the wood or in the soil and build mud tubes for protection.

- **Foraging Behavior:** Termites work around the clock, foraging through the wood and soil.

- **Colony Structure:** Termite colonies are large, with a complex caste system including workers, soldiers, and reproductive individuals.

Identification Tips for Homeowners

1. Inspect Physical Characteristics: Look closely at the size, color, and body shape of the insects. Carpenter ants are larger, and have a narrow waist, and bent antennae, while termites are smaller, and have a broad waist, and straight antennae.

2. Check for Wings: During swarming seasons, observe the wings of flying insects. Carpenter ants have wings of different lengths, whereas termites have wings of the same length.

3. Examine Nesting Signs: Carpenter ants leave behind sawdust-like frass near their nesting sites, which are smooth and free of mud. Termites, on the other hand, produce mud tubes and their galleries contain soil and debris.

4. Behavioral Observation: Note the foraging patterns. Carpenter ants are nocturnal foragers and are often seen in loose trails, while termites are constantly active and usually hidden from view.

5. Listen for Sounds: Sometimes you can hear rustling noises from termite activity within walls, whereas carpenter ants are less likely to make noticeable noise.

6. Damage Type: Inspect the type of damage. Carpenter ants create smooth tunnels in wood, while termite damage includes mud-lined tunnels and honeycomb patterns inside the wood.

Comparison Charts and Illustrations

Below is a detailed comparison chart to help differentiate carpenter ants from other ants and termites:

Feature	Carpenter Ants	Other Ants	Termites
Size	Workers: 6-12mm Queens: up to 20mm	Varies (typically smaller)	Workers: 3-4 mm, Swarmers: similar
Color	Bicolored: Red thorax, black abdomen	Varies (red, black, brown, etc.)	Pale white to light brown
Antennae	Bent (elbowed)	Bent (elbowed)	Straight (beaded)
Body Shape	Narrow waist with one node	Varies, typically with nodes	Broad waist, no noticeable segments
Wings	Front wings longer than rear wings	Similar to carpenter	Two pairs of equal-length wings

Nesting	In wood (hollowing It out)	Varies (Soil, wood, structures)	In wood and soil (consuming wood)
Foraging	Nocturnal, follow loose trails	Varies, day and night	Constant foraging, usually hidden
Frass	Produces sawdust-like material	Varies often no visible frass	Mud tubes, frass with soil/debris
Colony Structure	Multiple nests (main and satellites)	Varies (single or multiple nests)	Large colonies with a caste system
Behavior	Creates smooth galleries in wood	Varies	Creates mud tubes, honeycomb damage

The following are descriptions of what you should search for.

- Carpenter Ant Illustration:

  - Elbowed antennae

  - Narrow waist with one node

  - Larger body size

  - Smooth galleries in wood

- Termite Illustration:

  - Straight, beaded antennae

  - Broad waist, no segmentation

  - Equal length wings

  - Mud tubes and soil-lined galleries

- Other Ants Illustration:

  - Varying sizes and colors

  - Elbowed antennae

  - Nodes on the waist (one or two)

  - Different nesting habits

Advanced Studies and Future Research

Advanced Studies and Future Research

Current Research on Carpenter Ants

Research on Florida carpenter ants (Camponotus floridanus) has evolved significantly over recent years, with scientists delving into various aspects of their biology, behavior, and ecological impact. Current research topics include::

1. Amputation and Medical Treatment Behavior:

- The recent discovery of Florida carpenter ants performing amputations to save injured colony members has opened a new field of study. Researchers are focusing on the mechanisms and triggers for this behavior, the biochemical processes involved, and the evolutionary advantages it provides.

2. Communication and Social Structure:

- Carpenter ants exhibit complex communication systems primarily through pheromones. Studies are ongoing to decode these chemical signals, understand how they coordinate colony activities, and identify how these systems differ among ant species.

3. Nesting and Habitat Preferences:

- Researchers are examining the environmental factors that influence nesting site selection. This includes the role of moisture, wood decay, and competition with other species. Understanding these preferences helps in managing infestations and preserving natural habitats.

4. Foraging and Diet:

- Investigations into the foraging patterns and dietary preferences of Florida carpenter ants help to understand their role in the ecosystem. Studies focus on how these ants locate food, their interaction with other species, and the nutritional requirements of different colony members.

5. Genetics and Evolution:

- Genetic research aims to uncover the evolutionary history of carpenter ants and their adaptation to various environments. This includes studying the genetic basis for traits like amputation behavior, nesting preferences, and resistance to pathogens.

Potential Future Discoveries

As research on Florida carpenter ants progresses, several potential discoveries and areas of interest have emerged:

1. Advanced Medical Behaviors:

- Beyond amputation, there may be other sophisticated medical practices within ant colonies. Future research could uncover additional treatments for wounds, methods of disease prevention, and care for injured members that extend the current understanding of non-human medical behavior.

2. Ant-Plant Interactions:

- Understanding the symbiotic relationships between carpenter ants and plants, particularly those that provide food sources like honeydew-producing insects, could reveal more about the ecological balance and mutual benefits in these interactions.

3. Climate Change Impact:

- Studying how climate change affects the behavior, distribution, and survival of carpenter ants will be crucial. This includes examining how rising temperatures, changing precipitation patterns, and habitat loss influence their colonies and interactions with other species.

4. Behavioral Plasticity:

- Exploring the flexibility of carpenter ant behavior in response to environmental changes or stressors can provide insights into their resilience and adaptability. This research could inform pest management strategies and conservation efforts.

5. Inter-species Communication:

- Investigating how carpenter ants communicate and interact with other species, including predators, competitors, and mutualistic partners, could reveal complex networks of ecological relationships and survival strategies.

Importance of Continued Study

Continued research on Florida carpenter ants is vital for several reasons:

1. Ecological Understanding:

- Carpenter ants play a significant role in ecosystems as decomposers, predators, and prey. Understanding their behavior and interactions contributes to a broader knowledge of ecological dynamics and biodiversity.

2. Pest Management:

- Effective management of carpenter ant infestations in human habitats requires a deep understanding of their biology and behavior. Continued research can lead to improved control methods that are environmentally friendly and sustainable.

3. Biomimicry and Innovation:

- The sophisticated behaviors of carpenter ants, such as their medical treatments, can inspire innovations in technology and medicine. Studying these ants could lead to breakthroughs in robotics, healthcare, and other fields through the principles of biomimicry.

4. Conservation Efforts:

- Protecting carpenter ants and their habitats is crucial for maintaining ecological balance. Research can inform conservation strategies and help mitigate the impacts of human activities on these important insects.

5. Educational Value:

- Carpenter ants offer a fascinating subject for education and public engagement. Sharing research findings with a broader audience can foster an appreciation for insects, promote scientific literacy, and encourage future generations to pursue studies in entomology and ecology.

Conclusion

Florida carpenter ants are more than just a common pest; they are a window into the intricate and often surprising world of insect behavior and ecology. Advanced studies and future research hold the promise of uncovering even more remarkable aspects of these ants' lives, contributing to science, technology, and conservation. As we continue to explore their world, we gain a deeper appreciation for the complexity and interconnectedness of life on Earth.

CONCLUSION

Conclusion

Recap of Key Points

Throughout this book, we've explored the fascinating world of Florida carpenter ants (Camponotus floridanus), uncovering their remarkable behaviors, biology, and interactions with their environment. Here are the key points we've covered:

1. Remarkable Medical Discoveries:

- The discovery of amputation behavior in Florida carpenter ants is groundbreaking. These ants perform life-saving amputations on injured colony members, showcasing an advanced level of social care and medical treatment that is rare in the animal kingdom. This behavior involves the careful diagnosis of wounds and the execution of precise amputations to prevent infections and increase survival rates.

2. Basic Biology of Florida Carpenter Ants:

- Florida carpenter ants have distinctive physical characteristics, including their large size and reddish-black coloration. Their life-cycle consists of stages from egg to adult, with a lifespan that varies depending on the caste and environmental conditions. Seasonal behaviors, such as increased activity during warmer months, are driven by their need for food and suitable nesting sites.

3. Habitat and Nesting Habits:

- These ants prefer moist environments for nesting, often choosing decayed wood, attics, and other protected structures. Their nest-building activities can significantly impact both natural and human-made structures, sometimes leading to extensive property damage.

4. Diet and Foraging Behavior:

- Florida carpenter ants have a varied diet, including living and dead insects, sweets, and honeydew. Their nocturnal foraging patterns and interactions with other species, such as aphids, play a crucial role in their survival and ecological impact.

5. Infestations and Their Implications:

- Carpenter ant infestations can be identified by signs such as the presence of winged ants, frass, and visible damage to wood structures. These infestations can cause substantial economic and environmental consequences, necessitating effective management strategies.

6. Interaction with Humans:

- While Florida carpenter ants can bite, their bites are generally not harmful to humans. Understanding the myths and facts about these ants helps in managing their presence and reducing unnecessary fear.

7. Pest Control and Elimination:

- Effective methods for controlling carpenter ant infestations include eliminating moisture sources, sealing entry points, and using targeted treatments. Prevention tips and professional pest control solutions are essential for homeowners to protect their properties.

8. Differentiating Carpenter Ants from Other Ants and Termites:

- Identifying carpenter ants involves recognizing their unique physical and behavioral traits compared to other ants and termites. Homeowners can use comparison charts and illustrations to accurately differentiate these insects.

9. Advanced Studies and Future Research:

- Ongoing research on carpenter ants continues to reveal new insights into their behavior, genetics, and ecological roles. Future discoveries hold the promise of further understanding these complex insects and their interactions with the environment.

Final Thoughts on Florida Carpenter Ants

Florida carpenter ants are a testament to the incredible diversity and complexity of the natural world. Their advanced social behaviors, including the remarkable amputation treatment, highlight the sophistication of insect societies and the evolutionary adaptations that enable their survival. Studying these ants not only deepens our understanding of their biology but also provides broader insights into the functioning of ecosystems and the intricate relationships between species.

The discovery of their medical practices, particularly amputation, has significant implications for our understanding of animal behavior and evolution. It challenges us to rethink the capabilities of insects and the potential for sophisticated behaviors in seemingly simple organisms. This newfound knowledge opens up exciting possibilities for future research and innovations inspired by nature.

As we continue to explore the world of Florida carpenter ants, we gain a greater appreciation for their role in the environment and the delicate balance of ecosystems. Their presence in both natural and human-made habitats underscores the interconnectedness of life and the importance of studying and preserving biodiversity.

In conclusion, Florida carpenter ants are more than just pests; they are remarkable creatures with complex behaviors and significant ecological roles. By understanding and appreciating these ants, we can better coexist with them, manage their impacts, and continue to uncover the wonders of the natural world. This book serves as a comprehensive guide to the fascinating lives of Florida carpenter ants, shedding light on their mysteries and inspiring further exploration and discovery.

Appendices

Glossary of Terms

Amputation: The medical procedure of removing a limb or appendage. In the context of Florida carpenter ants, it refers to the behavior where ants amputate injured limbs of their colony members to prevent infection and increase survival rates.

Aphids: Small sap-sucking insects that are often farmed by ants for their honeydew, a sugary substance that aphids excrete. Aphids and ants have a mutualistic relationship where ants protect aphids from predators and in return, feed on the honeydew.

Autotomy: A defense mechanism in which an animal voluntarily sheds a part of its body, such as a tail or leg, to escape from a predator. This is different from the amputation behavior observed in Florida carpenter ants, where another ant performs the removal.

Brood: The eggs, larvae, and pupae stages in the life cycle of ants. The brood is cared for by worker ants and is essential for the growth and maintenance of the colony.

Camponotus floridanus: The scientific name for the Florida carpenter ant, a species known for its large size, reddish-black coloration, and unique medical behaviors like amputations.

Caste: The different forms of ants within a colony, each with specific roles. The primary castes include queens, males (drones), and workers. Workers can be further divided into minor and major workers based on size and function.

Formic Acid: A chemical compound produced by many ant species, including Florida carpenter ants, used for defense and as an antimicrobial agent. It is sprayed from the ant's abdomen to deter predators or sanitize wounds.

Frass: The fine sawdust-like material produced by carpenter ants when they excavate wood to build their nests. The presence of frass is a common sign of a carpenter ant infestation.

Honeydew: A sweet, sticky substance excreted by aphids and other plant-sucking insects. It is a favored food source for many ants, including Florida carpenter ants.

Infestation: The presence of a large number of pests, such as ants, within a structure or area. Infestations can lead to significant damage and require management and control measures.

Nuptial Flight: A mating flight in which winged male and female ants leave their colonies to mate. After mating, the males typically die, and the fertilized females establish new colonies.

Pheromones: Chemical signals produced by ants and other insects used for communication. Pheromones can mark trails, signal alarms, or indicate readiness to mate.

Pupa: The stage in an ant's life cycle between larva and adult. During the pupal stage, ants undergo metamorphosis, transforming into their adult forms.

Queen: The reproductive female in an ant colony. Queens are larger than worker ants and are responsible for laying eggs to ensure the colony's growth and survival.

Symbiosis: A firm and frequently long-term relationship between two distinct species. This is frequently used to describe mutualistic connections between ants and other insects, such as aphids.

Trophallaxis: The transfer of food or other fluids among members of a community through mouth-to-mouth or anus-to-mouth feeding. This behavior helps distribute nutrients and pheromones throughout the ant colony.

Worker Ant: Non-reproductive female ants are responsible for various tasks within the colony, such as foraging, caring for the brood, and defending the nest.

Workers can vary in size and are categorized as minors or majors based on their roles.

Winged Ants (Alates): Male and female ants that have wings and participate in the nuptial flight for reproduction. After mating, females lose their wings and establish new colonies, while males usually die shortly after mating.

www.ingramcontent.com/pod-product-compliance
Lightning Source LLC
Chambersburg PA
CBHW050829250726
48653CB00006B/2516